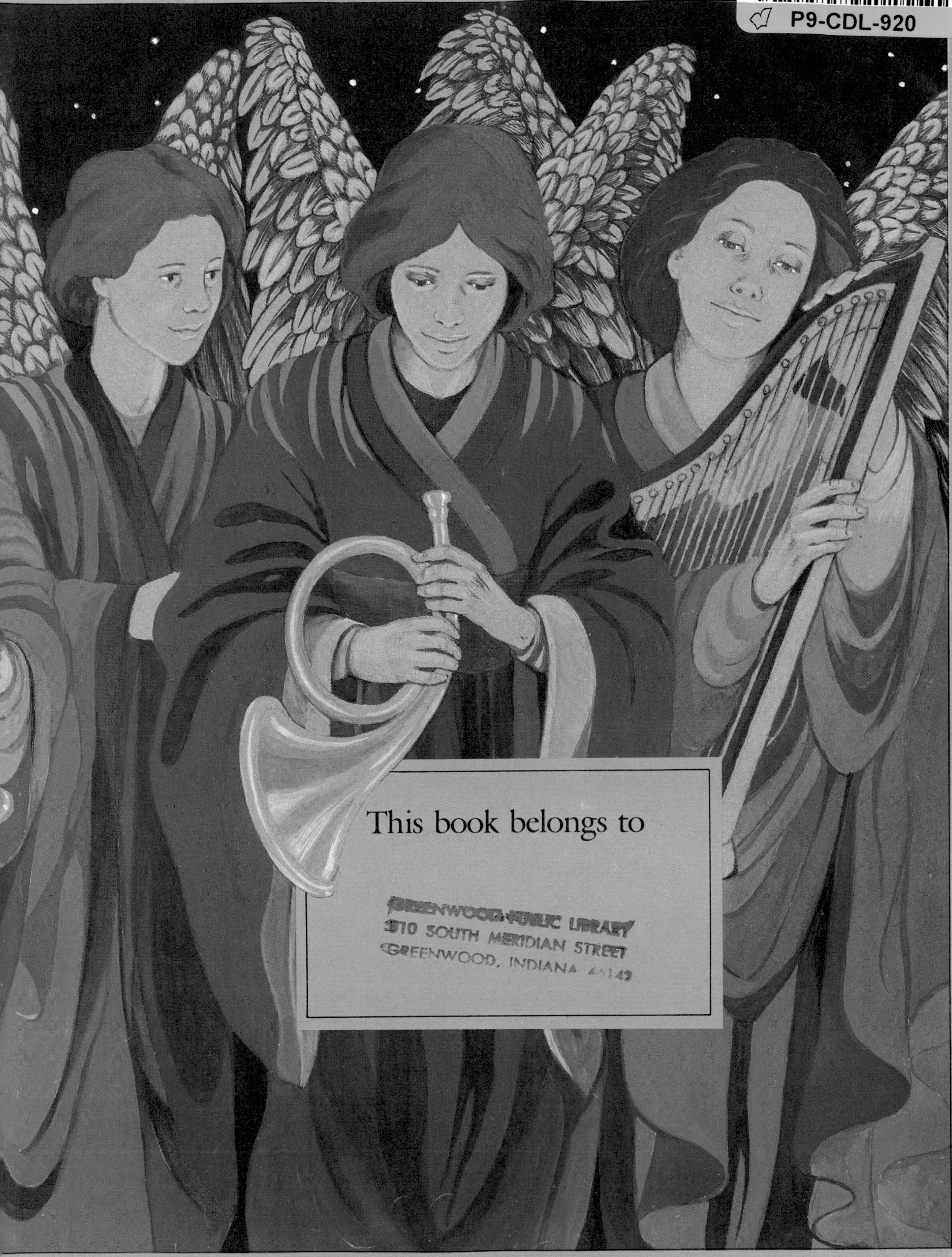
This book belongs to

SILENT NIGHT

illustrated by Susan Jeffers

verses by Joseph Mohr

E. P. Dutton   New York

Illustrations copyright © 1984 by Susan Jeffers

Published in the United States by E. P. Dutton, Inc.
2 Park Avenue, New York, N.Y. 10016

Published simultaneously in Canada by
Fitzhenry & Whiteside Limited, Toronto

Editor: Ann Durell   Designer: Isabel Warren-Lynch

Printed in the U.S.A.   COBE   First Edition
10 9 8 7 6 5 4 3 2 1

Library of Congress Cataloging in Publication Data
Mohr, Joseph, 1792–1848.
  Silent night.

  Translation of: Stille Nacht, heilige Nacht.
  Summary: An illustrated version of the well-known
German Christmas hymn celebrating the birth of Christ.
    1. Christmas music—Texts.   [1. Christmas music.
2. Hymns]   I. Jeffers, Susan, ill.   II. Title.
PZ8.3.M717Si   1984   783.6'52   84-8113
ISBN 0-525-44144-1

to my Auntie Rose and Uncle Tom

Silent night, holy night.

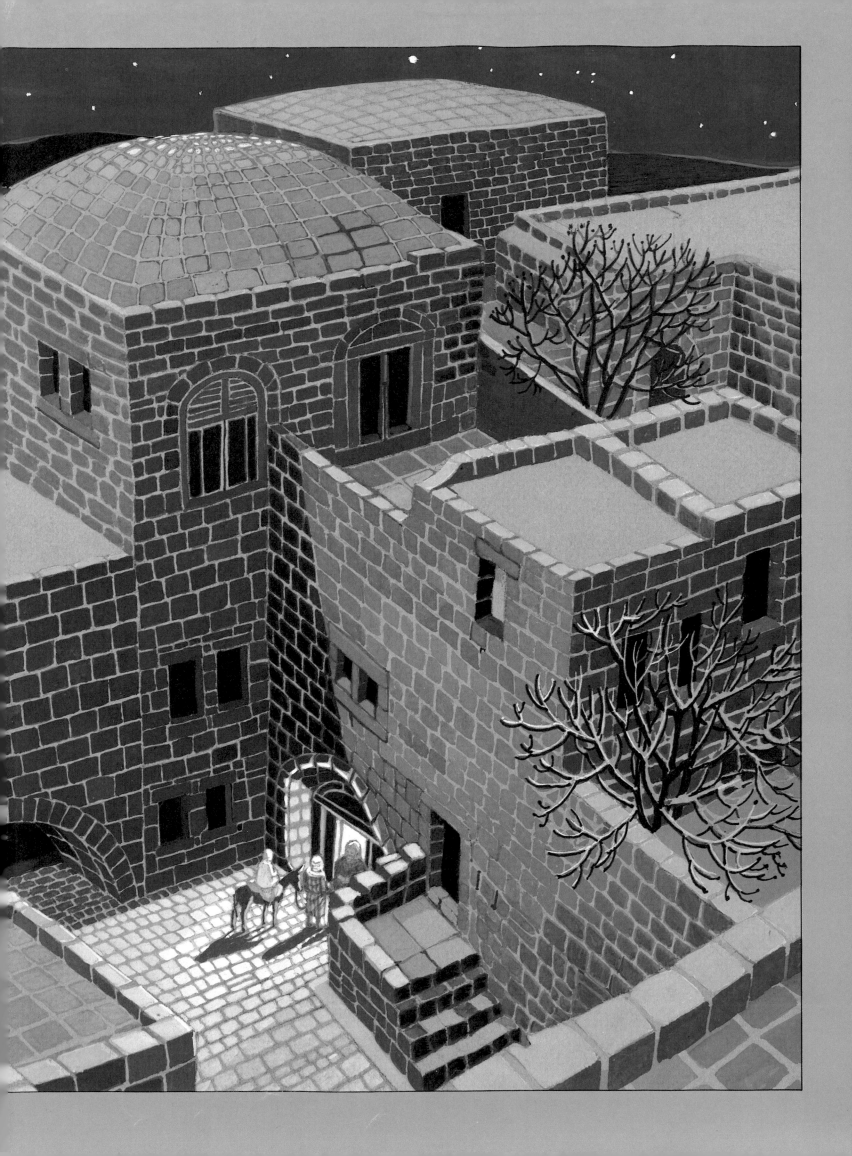

All is calm, all is bright
Round yon Virgin Mother and Child.
Holy Infant, so tender and mild,
Sleep in heavenly peace.

Sleep in heavenly peace.

Silent night, holy night!
Shepherds quake at the sight.
Glories stream from heaven afar.

Heav'nly hosts sing "Alleluia!"
Christ the Savior is born!
Christ the Savior is born!

Silent night, holy night!
Guiding star, lend thy light.

See the Eastern wise men bring
Gifts and homage to our King.

Christ the Savior is here!

Jesus the Savior is here!

Silent Night

verses by Joseph Mohr   music by Franz Gruber